# EARTH'S Immense OCEANS

### Isabel Thomas

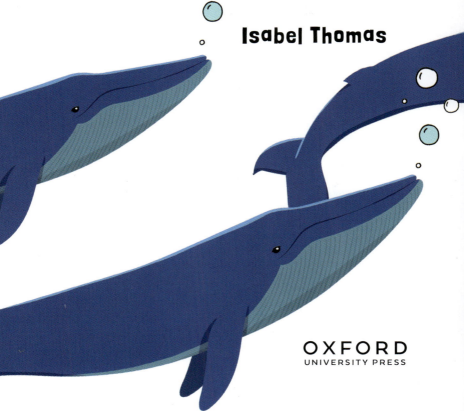

**OXFORD**
UNIVERSITY PRESS

Great Clarendon Street, Oxford OX2 6DP

Oxford is a registered trade mark of Oxford University Press
in the UK and in certain other countries

© Oxford University Press 2023
Text written by Isabel Thomas
Illustrated by Geraldine Sy and Ana Seixas

Designed and edited by Raspberry Books Ltd

The moral rights of the author and artist have been asserted
Database right Oxford University Press (maker)

First published 2023
This hardback edition published 2025

All rights reserved.

Library of Congress Cataloging-in-Publication Data is available.

ISBN 978-1-382-06651-8

1 3 5 7 9 10 8 6 4 2

Printed in China

The manufacturing process conforms to the
environmental regulations of the country of origin.

## Acknowledgments

The publisher and authors would like to thank the following for permission to use photographs and other copyright material:

**Cover:** Pavlo S/Shutterstock.
**Photos:** p1(tl): Pavlo S/Shutterstock; p5: Mclek/Shutterstock; p9: Mark Deeble and Victoria Stone/ Getty Images; p22: W. Scott McGill/Shutterstock; p24-25: Iavizzara/Shutterstock; p31: Nicku/Shutterstock; p46(t): Jan Martin Will/Shutterstock; p46(b): Ondrej ProsickyShutterstock; p47: Iakov Filimonov/Shutterstock; p53: Jesse Allen/NASA Earth Observatory; p58: rook76/Shutterstock; p59: Rich Carey/Shutterstock; p60: CarlsPix/Shutterstock; p62-63: World Digital Library; p65: Freshwater and Marine Image Bank; p66: Library of Congress, Geography and Map Division; p68: Slobodan Djajic/Shutterstock; p69: mariakray/Shutterstock; p71: NASA; p73: project1photography/Shutterstock; p74: Kiki Dohmeier/Shutterstock; p75(t): Shebeko/Shutterstock; p75(b): Jag_cz/Shutterstock; p76: Anteromite/Shutterstock; p77: NMC2S/Shutterstock; p78: Palo_ok/Shutterstock; p80: K3Star/Shutterstock; p81(t): Rvector/Shutterstock; p81(b): SoleilC/Shutterstock; p87: Matej Kastelic/Shutterstock; p91: Johan Larson/Shutterstock. **Front end paper:** pp2-3: Aleksandr Bryliaev/Shutterstock. **Back end paper:** p2: Pavlo S/Shutterstock.

Author photo courtesy of Isabel Thomas.

Artwork by **Geraldine Sy**, **Ana Seixas**, Ekaterina Gorelova, Adam Quest, and Oxford University Press.

Every effort has been made to contact copyright holders of material reproduced in this book. Any omissions will be rectified in subsequent printings if notice is given to the publisher.

**Images are to be used only within the context of the pages in this book.**

Did you know that we also publish Oxford's bestselling and award-winning **Very Short Introductions** series? These are perfect for adults and students
www.veryshortintroductions.com

# Contents

**Chapter 1.** Planet Ocean — 4
**Chapter 2.** How Oceans Work — 8
**Chapter 3.** Shaping the Planet — 20
**Chapter 4.** Life in the Oceans — 28
**Chapter 5.** Crossing the Oceans — 52
**Chapter 6.** Exploring the Depths — 62
**Chapter 7.** Using the Oceans — 72
**Glossary** — 92
**Index** — 95

# Chapter 1

# Planet Ocean

**The ocean covers almost three-quarters of Earth's surface, making it the largest habitat for plants and animals by a long way. To understand our planet, we must begin by understanding the ocean.**

Most of Earth's water is collected in five deep dips in the crust, the **ocean basins**. These **five great oceans** are connected to each other, and to about fifty smaller seas. Scientists often think of them as a single world ocean.

Scoop two pints of water from an ocean and you'll find around 1.2 oz. of **salts dissolved** in it. This is far saltier than two pints of fresh water from a river or lake. Salt water is **denser** than fresh water and freezes less easily—so ocean water can be colder than ice. But the most remarkable feature of the world's oceans is their mind-blowing size.

Together the **Arctic, Atlantic, Indian, Pacific, and Southern oceans** cover **almost 70% of the planet.** Their average depth is 2.3 miles (the height of Mount Everest from its base to its peak).

PLANET OCEAN

## Ocean names

The Indian and Southern oceans are named after their locations. The Atlantic Ocean is named after the ancient Greek god Atlas, who was forced to carry Earth's skies on his shoulders. The Pacific ("peaceful") Ocean was named by the explorer Ferdinand Magellan. The Arctic Ocean is named after the ancient Greek word for bear—the bears in question are constellations, or star patterns, that point toward the North Pole, which is always directly above this northernmost ocean.

The deepest point of any ocean is the **Challenger Deep of the Mariana Trench**, almost 6.8 miles below the surface.

EARTH'S IMMENSE OCEANS

## A world within a world

The salt water sloshing around in the oceans has a total volume of 321 million cubic miles (about a sixteenth of the volume of the Moon!). Life is thought to have begun in the oceans, and today they are home to every kind of living thing, from plants and animals to microbes. In total there are up to **10 million ocean species**—including the **very smallest** and the **very largest creatures on the planet.**

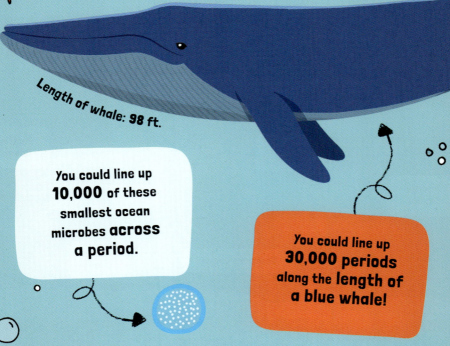

Length of whale: 98 ft.

You could line up **10,000** of these smallest ocean microbes **across a period.**

You could line up **30,000 periods** along the **length of a blue whale!**

As they go about their lives, ocean creatures capture **nutrients** such as carbon and nitrogen, and change them into forms that other living things use. In fact,

6

PLANET OCEAN

all living things on the planet depend on ocean life! The oceans also shape Earth's land, weather, and **climate**.

Humans have been using and exploring oceans for thousands of years. Today we can monitor oceans from up in space or travel down to the deepest depths. But much of this world within a world is still mysterious and unexplored.

In this very short introduction to Earth's oceans, you'll discover . . .

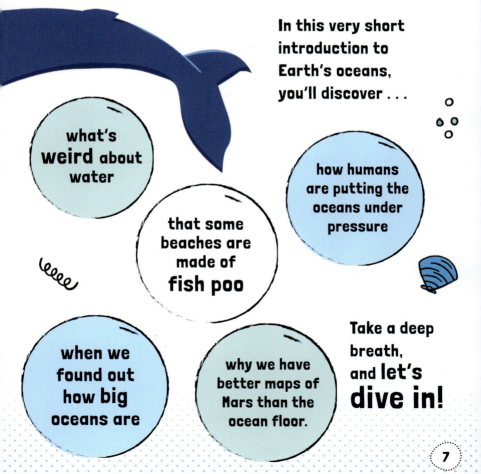

what's **weird** about water

that some beaches are made of **fish poo**

how humans are putting the oceans under pressure

when we found out how **big** oceans are

why we have better maps of Mars than the ocean floor.

Take a deep breath, and **let's dive in!**

7

# Chapter 2

# How Oceans Work

The weird properties of water help explain how oceans work—and how they got here in the first place.

**Molecules** of liquid water are strangely "sticky." They cling to each other, and it takes a lot of energy to break those bonds. This explains why liquid water flows long distances and collects in one place to form seas and oceans. It also explains why water can be found as a liquid, a solid, AND a gas at the kinds of temperatures we find naturally on Earth's surface—as you'll know if you've ever stepped on an ice-covered puddle.

Another unusual property of water is that it expands (takes up more space) when it freezes. Most substances do the opposite. As a result, solid water is less **dense** than liquid water, so ice floats on puddles—and oceans—instead of sinking. Most substances will change from liquid to solid if they are squeezed hard enough, but water bends this rule too. Even the water at the bottom of the Challenger Deep (the deepest part of the ocean) stays liquid, with 6.8 miles of water pressing down on it (the squeezing force of an entire hippo balanced on your fingernail!). This means that creatures can **live** in every **part of the ocean.**

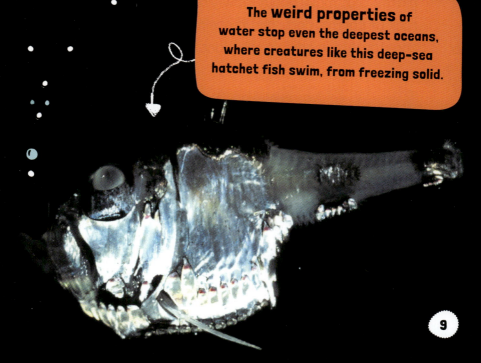

The **weird properties** of water stop even the deepest oceans, where creatures like this deep-sea hatchet fish swim, from freezing solid.

**EARTH'S IMMENSE OCEANS**

## Where did oceans come from?

Earth formed about **4.5 billion years ago**, but at first it was too hot for water to form. Water arrived later—some of it formed from oxygen and hydrogen that bubbled up from Earth's core and some was delivered by asteroids that crashed into the planet. As the planet cooled, this water vapor began to condense (turn to liquid) and the first rains fell, forming the first oceans.

## Oceans past, present, and future

Around 3 billion years ago there may have been no continents at all—just a few islands poking above water. But Earth's crust is split into huge **tectonic plates** that move about slowly on top of the molten rock of Earth's core, and these movements are constantly remodeling the planet.

**Inside Earth**

core

crust

mantle

**Earth around 2 billion years ago**

## HOW OCEANS WORK

Just 300 million years ago (not long compared to the age of Earth!) a supercontinent, known as Pangaea, had formed. The rest of the planet was covered by a vast ocean known as Panthalassa. Around 200 million years ago, Pangaea split into different pieces, which drifted into the positions of today's continents.

Pangaea

Panthalassa

Earth 300 million years ago

The size and shape of Earth's oceans is still changing, very slowly, as tectonic plates move about. For example, as plates under the Atlantic Ocean move apart, molten rock wells up to create new seabed. Sometimes, it also creates new land in the form of volcanic islands.

Every year, the Atlantic Ocean gets about 1.5 in. wider.

## Why are oceans blue?

Water absorbs (soaks up) sunlight, but the blue part of sunlight travels further through the water. As it travels, it gets bounced around. Some of this scattered light makes it back to the surface and escapes. This is the light that reaches our eyes, making the water appear blue.

EARTH'S IMMENSE OCEANS

# Why don't oceans dry up like puddles?

As water soaks up sunlight energy it warms up. This doesn't just make it more pleasant to swim on a sunny day—it gives water molecules at the surface the energy boost they need to break bonds with their neighbors and evaporate (turn to gas). This water vapor rises, cools, condenses, and falls as rain. Most rain that falls over land eventually trickles back to the oceans, topping them up, and the **water cycle starts again.**

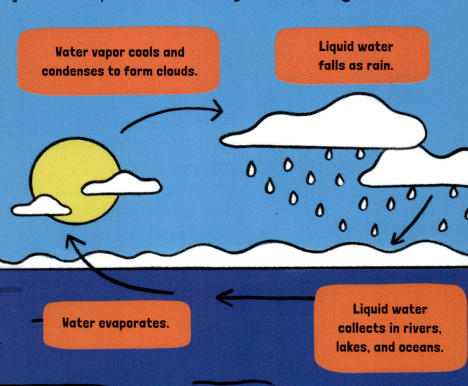

Water vapor cools and condenses to form clouds.

Liquid water falls as rain.

Water evaporates.

Liquid water collects in rivers, lakes, and oceans.

HOW OCEANS WORK

## Why are oceans salty?

As water flows across land, and through soil and rocks, **minerals** dissolve in it and get carried into the ocean too. Minerals also enter the water from volcanoes above and below the surface. These dissolved salts are left behind when the water evaporates, explaining why ocean water is so much saltier than fresh water. The main salt dissolved in seawater is **sodium chloride**—which is also **the salt we use on food.**

## Speak like a scientist

### DISSOLVE

Dissolving is a special kind of mixing. Solids get broken up into such tiny particles that they seem to disappear.

Oceans don't keep on getting saltier over time. Creatures that live in the oceans use dissolved minerals to build their bodies. This takes salts out of the water at the same rate they are being added, keeping the oceans in balance.

## Ocean in motion

The water in Earth's oceans is constantly on the move. It's easy to spot the rolling movement of waves, and the slow rise and fall of the tides. Harder to spot are powerful currents rushing up, down, and through the oceans like giant underwater rivers and waterfalls.

## How tides work

The tug of the Moon's gravity is strong enough to cause a "bulge" in Earth's oceans—on both sides of the planet. As Earth spins, this bulge of water sweeps over the oceans like a huge, never-ending wave. The regular change in water level is easiest to notice along the coasts, as tides.

When the **Sun, Earth, and Moon are lined up,** the effect of the Sun's gravity and the Moon's gravity make the difference between low and high tide greater than normal. This is known as a **spring tide**, because of the way the water seems to "spring" up! When the **Sun and Moon are at right angles,** tides are a little less dramatic than usual. These are known as **neap tides.**

The Earth and Moon move in a very regular way, so we can predict the timing of high and low tides.

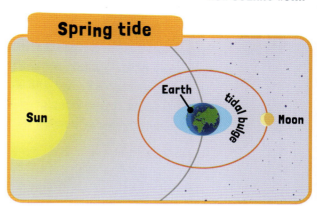

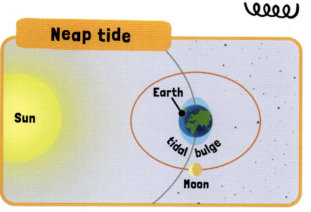

However, winds can change the height of tides along the coast, where the water is shallow.

Many plants and animals have adapted to life in **tidal habitats**.

Find out more on pages 30–33.

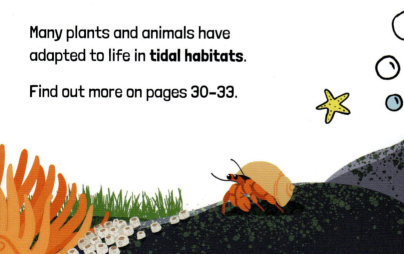

EARTH'S IMMENSE OCEANS

Waves don't move water from place to place—only **energy**. Like a stadium wave traveling through a crowd, the water in a particular spot just rises and falls in a circle as the energy passes through.

## How waves work

Waves begin when wind blows over open water. Thanks to **friction**, some of the movement energy of the wind is transferred to the water. Long after the force of the wind has gone, the energy is still being passed from one area of water to the next. The energy that makes water crash on to a shore might have been passed to the water days or weeks ago, by winds thousands of miles away.

HOW OCEANS WORK

**2** As waves enter **shallow water**, the **crests** are **forced closer** together and get **higher**.

**3** What happens **next** depends on the **energy of the wave** and the **shape of the shore**. Waves can **spill gently** onto a beach or **curl** and **break** with **a crash.**

**Bigger boosts** of energy—for example, from strong winds during a storm—cause **larger, more powerful waves.** The largest of all are known as tsunamis. These waves can travel as fast as a car and flatten buildings and trees as they wash over land. They are caused by sudden, violent movements of the ocean floor, such as an underwater earthquake, volcanic eruption or landslide, or a meteorite strike.

17

EARTH'S IMMENSE OCEANS

## How currents work

There are two main types of ocean currents. **Surface currents** are found near (you've guessed it) the ocean surface. Like waves, they're driven by the wind. Unlike waves, currents move both energy AND water from place to place.

The largest surface currents move in huge loops called gyres. They are shaped by the spinning of Earth in space, and by the land that gets in their way. Ocean gyres above and below the equator flow in opposite directions.

The North Atlantic Gulf Stream is one of the largest, strongest surface currents. It's a flow of water almost 100 times greater than the Amazon River, moving constantly from the warm Gulf of Mexico up the coast of North America and then across the Atlantic Ocean.

**Deep ocean currents** flow more slowly, driven by cooler, denser water sinking and flowing underneath warmer water. This flowing creates giant underwater waterfalls and rivers, where high density water flows through or underneath lower density water without the two mixing. The world's largest underwater waterfall, the Denmark Strait Cataract, lies hidden under the ocean between Greenland and Iceland. Every second, 123 million cubic feet of water plunges 2.17 miles into the North Atlantic Ocean.

HOW OCEANS WORK

## How the Denmark Strait Cataract works

warmer water

cooler, denser water

OVERFLOW

height of the **DENMARK STRAIT CATARACT**
2.17 mi. or 11,483 ft.

height of the **LARGEST WATERFALL**
0.6 mi. or 3,182 ft.

As waves CRASH, tides rise and fall and currents flow; energy, water, and things in the water get moved from place to place. This makes the oceans powerful forces for shaping our planet . . .

# Chapter 3

# Shaping the Planet

**Over the last 3.7 billion years, the ocean has changed from a superheated chemical "soup" to a habitat full of living things. Along the way it has shaped and reshaped the air, land, and life, in and out of the water!**

Scientists think life on Earth most likely began in the oceans. The first rains would have washed all kinds of chemicals into the oceans. A sudden boost of energy from a lightning storm caused simple chemicals such as water, hydrogen, ammonia, and methane to react together, and form more complicated molecules such as **amino acids**—the building blocks of living things. This idea has been tested and proven by scientists such as Cyril Ponnamperuma.

HOW OCEANS WORK

## OCEAN HERO

### CYRIL PONNAMPERUMA

Sri Lankan scientist who was one of the first to work out how life may have started in Earth's oceans.

In the 1970s, Cyril helped to work out that the first living things on the planet were tiny **plankton**, each made up of just one cell. Some of them evolved a mighty power—the ability to capture sunlight energy and use it to reassemble simple substances into food. This is called photosynthesis, and it's a superpower they later passed on to plants.

## Reshaping the planet

One of the waste products of photosynthesis is oxygen. Over time, **phytoplankton** burped out enough oxygen to completely change Earth's atmosphere. All kinds of new living things evolved to use this new, oxygen-rich air, including us!

## EARTH'S IMMENSE OCEANS

For most of this time, life on Earth was only found in the ocean. We know this because when we find fossils older than around 530 million years, they are in rocks that were once under the sea. In fact, many of these rocks were formed by the shells of dead sea creatures!

a megalodon tooth

Life in the oceans has changed over time. **We have found fossils of thousands of strange sea creatures that are now extinct**, such as **the giant shark, megalodon.**

Around 500 million years ago, certain ocean creatures began leaving the water for a short time—perhaps to find a safe place to lay eggs. A hundred million years later, the first land plants joined in—and quickly took over. Plants have changed the atmosphere and created habitats where a huge range of animals and other living things can survive away from the water. But **all life on land has ancestors that lived in the oceans.**

22

**SHAPING THE PLANET**

The very **first animals** with **backbones were bony fish.** They are the ancestors of all the **vertebrates** we see around us, from birds and crocodiles to mammals.

Over time, some land animals adapted to spend some (or all) of their time in ocean habitats—evolving into today's **marine mammals** and reptiles.

*You humans are just fish that have adapted to live on land.*

## Shaping the climate

Today the ocean "soup" is more complex and nutritious than ever. Billions of tons of minerals are dissolved in the oceans, including carbon dioxide from the air. Today's phytoplankton capture energy from sunlight and use it to break apart carbon dioxide to build their bodies.

When the phytoplankton are eaten by larger creatures, the captured carbon is passed up the food chain—and eventually sinks to the bottom when ocean animals poop, sink, or die. This "locks" carbon into the deep ocean, meaning there is much less carbon dioxide in the atmosphere than there would otherwise be. Carbon dioxide is one of the main **greenhouse gases**, so ocean life helps keep the planet cooler.

## Shaping the weather

Waves, tides, and currents transfer vast amounts of energy across Earth's surface, which shapes weather patterns and helps control local climates. Ocean waters warmed by the sun provide the energy and water vapor that fuel storm systems. These continually bring fresh water back to land in the form of rain.

Gigantic, spiraling storms form over oceans that have been warmed by the sun.

## Shaping coasts

The oceanic crust, deep below the ocean, is made of a different, denser type of rock from those that form continents. Both types float on top of the molten rock of Earth's mantle, in the same way that icebergs float in water or toys float in the bath. Continental crust floats higher, which is why it forms land. As ocean water moves about, it constantly reshapes this land.

### Speak like a scientist

**SEDIMENTS**

Sediments are solid particles that have made their way into the oceans, for example, sand or mud washed into the ocean by rivers. Sediments sink in water but get churned up and moved around by waves and currents.

## EARTH'S IMMENSE OCEANS

Waves and tides carry sediments from place to place. They can deposit sand on a shore and create a beach, or cause pebbles to drift away over time. They can smash sediments against cliffs, wearing the rock away, eroding and reshaping coasts over time.

## HOW COASTLINES CHANGE

1.

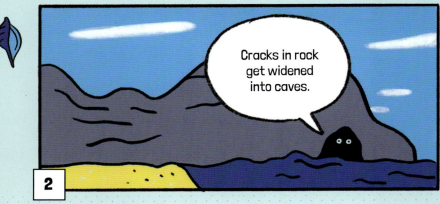

2.

**SHAPING THE PLANET**

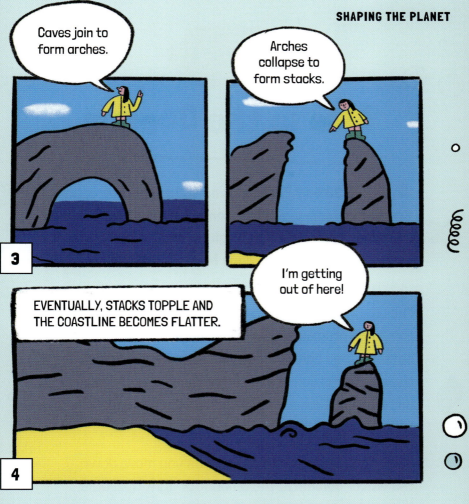

Beaches form from whichever sediments happen to be nearby. Black sands are made from volcanic rocks broken apart by the churning of waves. The white sands of tropical beaches are made from dead coral pooped out by parrotfish!

Let's **explore** more of the extraordinary ocean creatures that **shape** our planet in surprising ways.

# Chapter 4

# Life in the Oceans

More than 90% of Earth's living space is in the oceans. Creatures from every kingdom of life are found in and around them, including bright orange sea slugs and crabs the size of cars. Many have no relatives on land.

The oceans are not like enormous fish tanks, where the same creatures explore the water from top to bottom. They contain many different habitats, and the creatures found in a rock pool or reef are very different to those living in the deep, dark ocean trenches.

One of the biggest differences as you move down the **water column** is the amount of light available. **Near the surface**, sunlight warms the water.

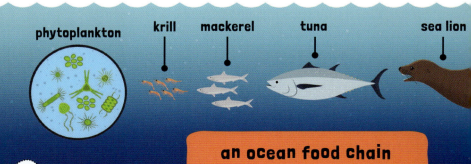

an ocean food chain

**LIFE IN THE OCEANS**

Phytoplankton and seaweeds use the energy in sunlight to capture carbon and make their own food. Like plants on land, they are eaten by animals, and energy and nutrients **pass up the food chain**.

Together, the animals living in the world's oceans weigh around three times more than all the animals living on land. Most ocean animals are fish or **arthropods** (animals with a hard outer skeleton and a body in segments, such as krill, crabs, or barnacles).

Even in the clearest seas, only 1% of light makes it more than a few hundred yards below the surface. **In the deeper ocean**, creatures must rely on food drifting down from above—as well as other sources of energy and nutrients. Some have evolved incredible adaptations to enable them to live in extreme conditions that would harm most other living things.

Let's explore some ocean ecosystems and the creatures that call them home.

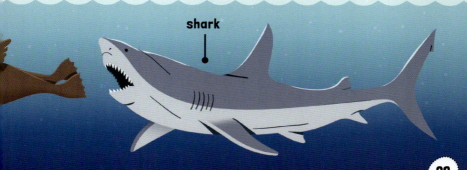

shark

EARTH'S IMMENSE OCEANS

# Rocky coasts

Many ocean creatures make their homes where ocean meets land. As waves crash on the shore and tides ebb and flow, rocks in this zone are covered with water for part of each day but exposed to sunlight and air for the rest.

Rock pools stay flooded with water when the tide goes out, but also with light. They are often crowded with life. At the bottom of rock pool food chains are **algae**. Seaweeds are huge algae, with the power to capture energy from sunlight. Unlike plants, they can cling to rocks without needing roots. Lichens are a **hybrid** of two living things—tiny algae living inside a **fungus**! The algae get protection and share the food they make with the fungus.

30

**LIFE IN THE OCEANS**

Many rock pool animals are also fixed in one place. Jelly-like sea anemones pull in their tentacles for protection, or pop them out to catch passing food. Barnacles were made famous by Charles Darwin. Inside each barnacle is a tiny **crustacean**, waiting for high tide. When the water returns, they pop out their feathery limbs and comb the water for food.

Mollusks such as snails and limpets, and **echinoderms** such as sea stars (also known as starfish) and sea urchins, graze on the rocks, scraping off algae and bacteria.

## OCEAN HERO

### CHARLES DARWIN

**Nineteenth-century British naturalist, best known for explaining how living things evolve. He was also a marine biologist and world expert on barnacles.**

EARTH'S IMMENSE OCEANS

## Muddy shores

Along estuaries, fresh river water meets salt water from the ocean. As the rushing river water suddenly slows, sediments it carried sink and settle in thick layers. They may form muddy shores, known as mudflats, which are bathed by salt water at least twice a day. On some muddy shores, plants such as grasses and mangroves find a way to anchor themselves in the mud. They form unique habitats, such as salt marshes and mangrove swamps, which soon become home to other living things.

Most plants can't live in salty conditions because water likes to flow from less salty to more salty places. So water would flow out of the plants' roots instead of in! Salt marsh plants have adapted to store salt in their leaves, so water

32

**LIFE IN THE OCEANS**

moves in the right direction. Mangrove trees are also adapted to live in salty water. Their roots spread wide to keep the trees stable on soft, muddy, flooded ground. Tiny creatures make their home on the roots, and larger animals such as crabs and lizards hide in between.

## Life in the mud

Imagine living your whole life hidden in mud! This is reality for many bivalves—mollusks with two-part shells. The edge of their shell pokes out, sucking in water and filtering tiny particles of food. However, being good at hide and seek is no guarantee of safety. Shorebirds that live along muddy coasts have bills adapted for digging up hidden worms and mollusks.

Cockles have a muscly "foot" to burrow into sand or mud.

Some shore animals have adapted by developing better armor! The mangrove horseshoe crab has dome-shaped armor, scissor-tipped claws, and a spiky "tail" to flip itself over.

33

# Seagrass meadows

Near the coast, shallow ocean water is flooded with light. The water is also rich in nutrients that wash off the land or well up from the deep ocean. No wonder so much life gathers here—including plants. Like land plants, seagrasses have flowers, seeds, and roots anchored in the sand.

These underwater meadows provide food and hiding places for animals such as crabs and jellyfish. Water supports the weight of ocean animals, so crustaceans such as lobsters and crabs can get much bigger than their cousins on land.

Seagrass meadows also attract huge schools of fish that come to eat plankton, and larger animals that feast on the smaller animals. Working in the twentieth century, marine biologist Eugenie Clark revealed that even

## OCEAN HERO

### EUGENIE CLARK

**American scientist who studied fish and became known as "Shark Lady."**

## LIFE IN THE OCEANS

animals at the top of the food chain, such as sharks, are a vital part of these fragile ocean ecosystems.

Together, seagrass meadows cover an area larger than the size of California! They absorb lots of carbon dioxide from the water, storing the carbon in their leaves. They also protect coastlines from storms and tides, by absorbing some of the energy of waves.

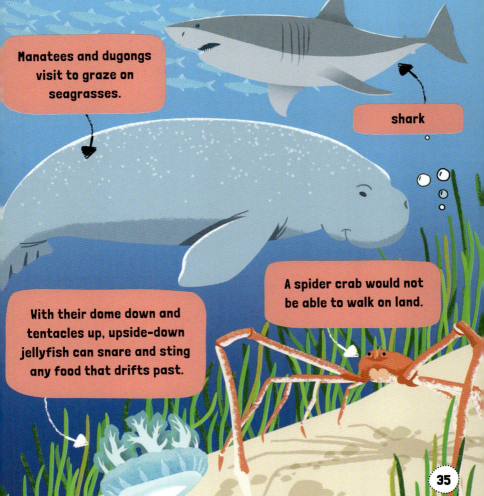

Manatees and dugongs visit to graze on seagrasses.

shark

A spider crab would not be able to walk on land.

With their dome down and tentacles up, upside-down jellyfish can snare and sting any food that drifts past.

EARTH'S IMMENSE OCEANS

## Kelp forests

Like plants, seaweeds have green **pigments** to capture the sun's energy for photosynthesis. Some seaweeds have extra pigments to absorb more colors of light—these red seaweeds can grow in deeper waters.

Giant kelp are the largest seaweeds of all. Their fronds grow up to 100 ft. long, forming underwater forests. Tiny gas-filled "balloons" keep the kelp floating upright, with no need for a trunk. Sea urchins graze on the kelp. Like starfish, they are echinoderms, but with long spines between their tube feet! Sea otters live among the kelp and eat sea urchins. They wrap kelp strands around their front legs to anchor themselves in place as they doze, so they don't drift to shore (where there are predators) or out to sea.

**LIFE IN THE OCEANS**

Kelp forests are visited by other land animals too. Marine iguanas are the only lizards to find their food at sea. They swim differently from other lizards, with a butterfly movement. Their swimming and diving skills help them feed on algae growing underwater.

If you could weigh every living thing on land, the total weight of the plants at the bottom of the food chain would be many times more than all the animals that depend on them for food. This makes sense. But amazingly, in the oceans, the opposite is true! The ocean's phytoplankton and seaweeds weigh far less than all the animals they support. It's possible because phytoplankton and seaweeds can capture sunlight energy and carbon and grow much faster than plants on land do. Giant kelp can grow more than 23 in. in a single day!

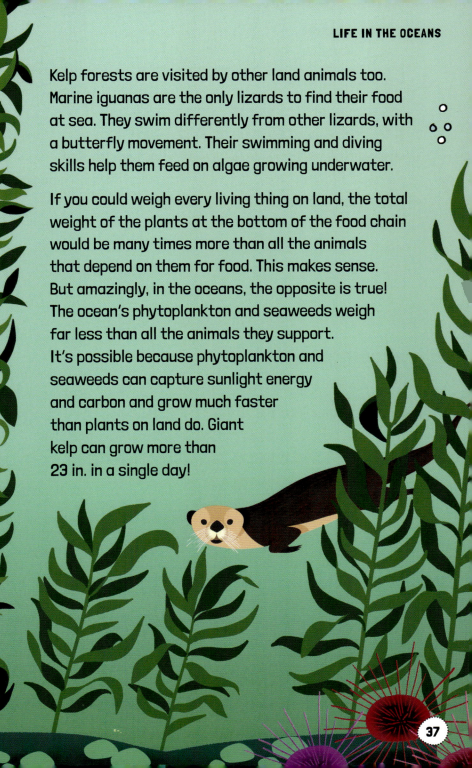

## Coral reefs

Coral reefs are built by tiny animals called **coral polyps**—like sea anemones, but with better engineering skills! They live in large communities of millions, feeding on plankton by trapping them in their tentacles. As the coral polyps grow, they use the calcium carbonate from the planktons' shells to build themselves a tiny, hard home—like a skeleton they can pop in and out of. When a polyp dies, its hard home is left behind and new polyps build their homes on top. Over millions of years, the reef slowly grows.

## Working together

Today, coral reefs are home to a quarter of all types of sea creature on the planet! This includes a third of the world's fish species. In these crowded underwater cities of the sea, bright colors help tropical fish signal which species they belong to.

Living on a reef means LOTS of competition for food and hiding places. So, some reef creatures team up to get ahead, living in **symbiosis**. Cleaner shrimps

## LIFE IN THE OCEANS

hop on and off larger creatures, eating their parasites and dead skin. Yum! Clownfish hide among the stinging tentacles of sea anemones. Giant clams and polyps provide a home for phytoplankton that make their food using the energy in sunlight. In return for protection, the phytoplankton share the food they make with the clams and polyps.

When two different species live closely together (sometimes one even lives inside the other!) and cooperate, each one benefits.

Larger predators flock to reefs to look for food, so many smaller reef creatures have evolved good defenses!

**Turn the page to see some examples of those defenses in action.**

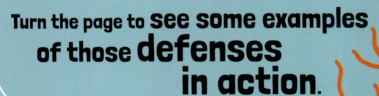

Hey, wait for me!

39

EARTH'S IMMENSE OCEANS

# Open oceans

Towering waves, strong currents, and a lack of hiding places make the open ocean a tough place to live.

In the sunlit zone near the surface, every drop of water contains thousands of algae and **cyanobacteria** that can make their own food by photosynthesis. Together they are known as phytoplankton.

Tiny animals (known as zooplankton) feed on the light-harvesting phytoplankton. Fish, jellyfish, and other animals come to the surface to feed on both types of plankton, and larger fish and marine mammals in turn come to feed on those.

There are many different kinds of phytoplankton. Some form beautiful hard shells, which can only be seen under a microscope.

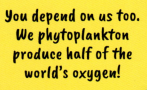

You depend on us too. We phytoplankton produce half of the world's oxygen!

LIFE IN THE OCEANS

## OCEAN HERO

### ALFRED REDFIELD

**Made amazing discoveries about nutrients in the ocean.**

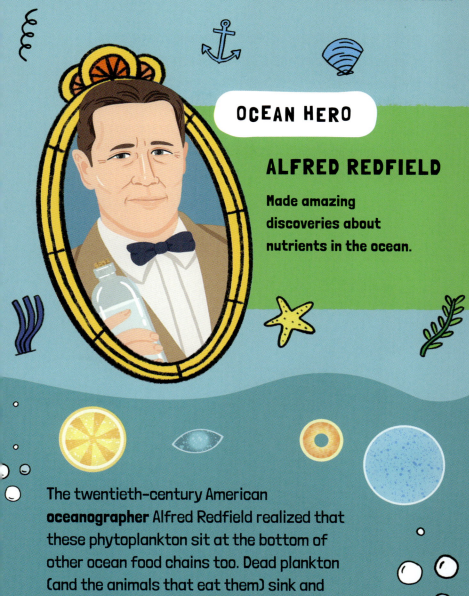

The twentieth-century American **oceanographer** Alfred Redfield realized that these phytoplankton sit at the bottom of other ocean food chains too. Dead plankton (and the animals that eat them) sink and become a source of energy and nutrients for creatures living deep below the surface.

## EARTH'S IMMENSE OCEANS

At times, the ocean surface becomes a feeding frenzy. In large schools of fish, each fish matches its movements to its nearest neighbor, so the whole school turns, darts, and dives together in a synchronized way. The fish avoid crashing into each other, and each fish blends into the crowd, so it's less likely to be snapped up by a predator.

Why are fish so smart?

**LIFE IN THE OCEANS**

Jellyfish belong to a group of ocean animals called **cnidarians**, which includes corals and anemones. They have long stinging tentacles to catch prey. The largest is the lion's mane jellyfish, which can snare fish and crustaceans. Large fish rely on bursts of speed to catch prey. Sailfish and swordfish are the speediest animals in the sea, breaking the 60 mph barrier—which is almost as fast as cheetahs can run on land! They stun smaller fish by sweeping their long bills quickly through the water, making the prey easier to catch.

Seabirds swoop down in feeding frenzies to catch the fish. Many seabirds feed in the open ocean, and some fly hundreds of miles from land. The albatross can stay at sea for years and can even drink salty water, which would harm most birds.

Filter-feeding whales are the largest creatures in the open ocean—and anywhere on Earth! They feed on some of the smallest creatures, catching them in sieve-like **baleen** plates by swimming along with their mouths open.

Because we're always in school!

EARTH'S IMMENSE OCEANS

## Polar oceans

The Arctic Ocean is the world's smallest ocean. At the opposite end of the world, the Southern Ocean surrounds the huge continent of Antarctica. These oceans get less energy from the sun, so are colder than other oceans. They are always partly covered in floating ice. The amount of sea ice, and the pattern of life, changes with the seasons.

In the summer, huge swarms of phytoplankton and krill provide a feast for fish, seals, whales, penguins, and squid, which in turn are prey for huge marine mammals such as orcas and polar bears.

penguin

### ✸ Speak like a scientist ✸

# KRILL

Krill are tiny crustaceans found in vast swarms in all the world's oceans. They are the main food for many polar animals.

seal

**LIFE IN THE OCEANS**

orca

Family groups (pods) of orcas are found in both of the polar oceans and everywhere in between, a wider range than any other marine mammal. They catch and eat pretty much anything—turtles, jellyfish, huge sea lions, and dolphins—giving them their nickname "killer whales." Each pod focuses on a particular type of prey, using hunting techniques and teamwork that they teach their young.

## Staying warm

The huge marine mammals that live in the polar oceans have a thick layer of fat under their skin called blubber. It stops their body heat escaping and also acts as an energy store for the winter, when there is less food to be found.

Fish can't make their own body heat, so many polar fish make chemicals to stop them freezing!

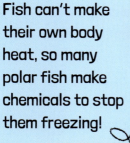

polar bear

EARTH'S IMMENSE OCEANS

## The abyssal zone

Thousands of feet below the ocean surface, across abyssal plains and in deep-sea trenches, most living things would be killed by the crushing pressure of the water above, cold temperatures, and total darkness. But many sea creatures thrive here.

## Speak like a scientist

### ABYSSAL PLAINS

These are the vast, flat areas of sea floor between 1.8 and 3.7 miles under the ocean surface. They cover around half of the planet. They are covered in a deep layer of muddy sediments washed off the land.

Light-harvesting creatures don't live in the ocean depths—they can't make food without light. So instead of eating plants or phytoplankton, many deep-sea creatures, such as sea cucumbers, are **detritivores** that eat "marine snow." This is more disgusting than it sounds—a mixture of droppings and dead creatures that drifts down from above! Animals of the abyssal plains grow slowly and live long lives—

**LIFE IN THE OCEANS**

so can become very large. They include giant isopods, like pink-armored woodlice the size of a school ruler.

## Glow in the dark

An amazing nine out of ten deep-sea creatures create their own light—a trick called **bioluminescence**. Chemical reactions in their bodies (often carried out by resident bacteria) produce a soft glow. The light is used to confuse predators or attract prey or mates.

EARTH'S IMMENSE OCEANS

## Deep hydrothermal vents

Hydrothermal vents are hot springs where water heated by molten rocks gushes constantly out of cracks in the sea floor. The hot water contains so many dissolved minerals it can look white or black.

When scientists first discovered hydrothermal vents around forty years ago, they were amazed to find huge numbers of animals living around them. Very little sinking food from the surface reaches these deepest parts of the oceans, so what on earth were they eating? They soon discovered that food chains around hydrothermal vents rely on a **totally different source of energy and nutrients . . . Bacteria!**

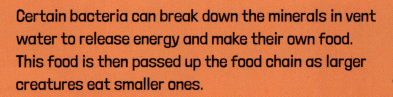

Certain bacteria can break down the minerals in vent water to release energy and make their own food. This food is then passed up the food chain as larger creatures eat smaller ones.

Many deep-sea vent creatures **look more like aliens than animals.** For example, most have **no eyes**—growing them would be a waste of energy. They may show us what life on **distant moons and planets could look like!**

# Crossing the Oceans

**For some creatures, the oceans are impassable barriers. For others, they are routes to new homes. This helps to explain why certain plants and animals are found in some places but not others. Oceans have also shaped human history.**

Earth's land was once part of a single supercontinent—explaining why similar fossils of creatures, such as dinosaurs and **marsupials**, are found thousands of miles apart, on different land masses.

As the supercontinent Pangaea (see page 11) broke up and drifted apart over millions of years, vast oceans opened between continents. Most land plants and animals cannot survive in salt water, so for millions of years, creatures on distant continents have evolved separately, without mixing.

For example, Australasia and the Americas were once joined by a forest-covered Antarctica, but became separated by oceans around 40 million years ago. Over this time, most marsupials living in the Americas became extinct. But the marsupials that found

**CROSSING THE OCEANS**

themselves in Australia were very successful. Many new species evolved that are found nowhere else in the world.

In contrast, some **microbes**, plant seeds, and animals can fly, float, or swim across oceans—an adaptation that helps them find new homes.

The island known as Hunga Tonga-Hunga Ha'apai formed during a volcanic eruption in 2014. Just a few years later it is already home to birds that have flown from nearby islands, and plants that have grown from seeds in bird droppings!

the island called **Hunga Tonga-Hunga Ha'apai**

## EARTH'S IMMENSE OCEANS

At first, humans could not cross oceans. They were simply a source of food and materials for people who lived near coasts. Archaeologists have found traces of barbecued shellfish left in caves by Stone Age humans around 164,000 years ago!

This handy source of food may have helped humans gradually migrate from Africa, where the first humans lived, to new parts of the world. As rafts and rowing boats were invented, prehistoric humans were able to migrate to distant places.

Traditional stories show **how important the oceans** were to **coastal communities**—as a source of food, and as something to be feared and respected.

**CROSSING THE OCEANS**

This is how the first humans reached the continent that is now Australia and New Guinea, around 47,000 years ago, probably voyaging from island to island until they had covered a great distance.

The first sailing vessels were made around 7,000 years ago, allowing people to catch fish further out at sea and to explore further from home. Sailing ships (armed with weapons) allowed civilizations to build and control huge empires. From ancient times onward, human history has been closely linked to the ability to cross oceans. States that were powerful at sea would trade with, or even just raid, other places, and stop others from attacking them. For example, being able to travel and trade at sea, and control important ports, helped ancient Egypt stay rich and powerful for thousands of years.

EARTH'S IMMENSE OCEANS

In the 1400s, Western European countries began competing to discover and control quicker sea routes to places that had once only been reached by land.

Crossing oceans in sailing ships was dangerous, and shipwrecks were common, but sailors hoped for adventure and riches. Their tales of peril inspired myths and legends, often involving **great ocean monsters such as the Kraken.**

**CROSSING THE OCEANS**

Many of these stories were probably based on glimpses of real ocean creatures, such as colossal squid or narwhals, said to be "unicorns of the sea."

At this point, explorers were not that interested in the ocean itself—it was just something to cross to see what was on the other side. However, the fierce competition to cross oceans did help people to learn more about the world. It led explorers from Western Europe to land on the shores of the Americas, and later Australia—places they had not known were there.

In the sixteenth century, the Portuguese explorer Ferdinand Magellan led the first known voyage all the way around the world, setting off to the west and returning from the east. This proved that Earth was a sphere and put the Pacific Ocean on European maps for the first time.

These expeditions across oceans shaped the world for centuries to come, and often had a terrible impact on the peoples already living in these places. For example, when the British Captain Cook landed in Australia in 1770, it was home to around 750,000 **Indigenous** Australians, peoples who had lived there for thousands of years. Within twenty years, 90% of Indigenous Australians had died because of diseases introduced by British colonists, conflict, and being displaced from their lands.

EARTH'S IMMENSE OCEANS

# The darkest days

The mid-1500s to the mid-1800s was an age of sail, where tall ships criss-crossed the world's oceans carrying cargo. It was also one of the darkest times in human history, when millions of people were taken from their homes in African countries and sold into slavery—often on the other side of the Atlantic Ocean. It is impossible to measure the impact of the **transatlantic slave trade** on both the people taken and the countries they were stolen from.

It's estimated that over the course of 300 years, more than 17 million African people were stolen and shipped across the Atlantic Ocean to the Americas. Around 2 million victims died as they crossed the ocean due to the terrible treatment and conditions on the ships. These ships then returned to Europe carrying goods such as sugar, cotton, and coffee, produced with slave labor. Then the ships returned to Africa, to repeat the journey over and over again.

### The transatlantic slave trade

- sugar, tobacco, and cotton to Europe
- textiles, rum, and manufactured goods to Africa
- enslaved people to the Americas

CROSSING THE OCEANS

# Hunting whales

People have hunted whales for thousands of years but from the seventeenth to early nineteenth century, whaling became one of the most important industries in the world. As whaling crews roamed the world, they gained new knowledge of the oceans but they also **decimated** many populations of Earth's largest animals.

Nearly every part of a whale was sold to make things:

Whale **meat** was eaten.

Bendy **baleen** was used to make **roofing**, **baskets**, **splints** for broken bones, and fashionable clothes.

Whale **oil** and **blubber** were used to make **soap**, burned in lamps, and used to grease the mighty **machines** of the Industrial Revolution.

Whale **bones** were carved into **tools** and **ornaments**.

**Ambergris** was used to make expensive **perfume**.

The **hooped skirts** fashionable in the 1700s and 1800s were made from cotton and baleen, products of the **slave trade** and **whaling**.

59

EARTH'S IMMENSE OCEANS

## The first oceanographers

Trade ships were joined in the oceans by hundreds of navy ships, which protected the cargo ships and controlled important routes. Navies also looked for ways to make sea voyages faster, more accurate, and less deadly. They did this by learning about winds, currents, tides, and depths in different parts of the ocean—and using this information to find better routes.

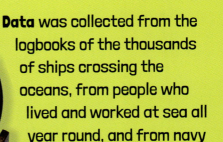

**Data** was collected from the logbooks of the thousands of ships crossing the oceans, from people who lived and worked at sea all year round, and from navy ships themselves.

Even by the end of the 1800s, hundreds of ships were still being wrecked when they became grounded on rocks or stranded on coasts. The race to get better at navigation led to the invention of new devices such as **the chronometer, the first portable timekeeping device.**

marine chronometer

CROSSING THE OCEANS

## Crossing with cables

The maps and charts created by navies also helped to plan a route for the first **telecommunications** cable to cross the Atlantic Ocean. When this was laid in 1865, it allowed information to be sent quickly from Europe to North America for the first time. Before that, news and messages could only be carried across the ocean on ships, which took weeks or months!

Today, we take ocean cables for granted. Ninety-nine per cent of internet and other data sent around the world travels through these underwater bundles of wires and glass fibers,

**zipping** under the oceans in **seconds.**

## Chapter 6

# Exploring the Depths

**For most of human history, people had little idea what lay below the ocean surface. The scientific study of the oceans changed this, beginning a quest to explore the deep seas that is still happening.**

Old maps of the ocean are packed with monsters thought to lurk beneath the waves. For thousands of years, people considered the deep ocean a mysterious and dangerous place where a shipwreck could result in being eaten by sharks—or worse!

**EXPLORING THE DEPTHS**

At first, people focused on working out how to cross the ocean surface as quickly as possible to reach land on the other side. They didn't think anything could possibly live in the cold, dark water below the sunlit surface, and especially not on the seabed. But gradually, this changed.

When broken cables were pulled to the surface, people were amazed to see them covered in strange living things! Then, in 1868, a ship dredging (scraping) the sea floor **more than 2.5 miles deep**, brought sea creatures to the surface.

Increasingly, the oceans seemed like interesting places to explore. Perhaps even places where valuable things could be found. The race was on to find out more about the ocean depths and the creatures that lived there.

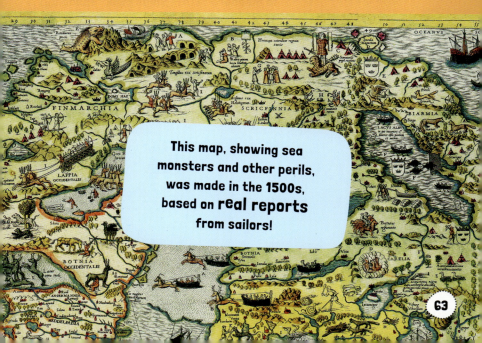

This map, showing sea monsters and other perils, was made in the 1500s, based on **real reports** from sailors!

EARTH'S IMMENSE OCEANS

# Hidden life

In 1872, an old navy ship called *HMS Challenger* set off on a three-and-a-half-year mission: to measure the depth of the seabed and take samples from the bottom of every large ocean. On board was a team of six scientists led by marine biologist Charles Wyville Thomson, armed with tools to measure things like the saltiness of the water (salinity) and temperature.

> To measure depth, ships took "soundings" by dropping a lead weight attached to a line into the water. Markers were tied on to the line and counted as it disappeared below the waves.

EXPLORING THE DEPTHS

## OCEAN HERO

### CHARLES WYVILLE THOMSON

Scottish naturalist who helped persuade the Royal Navy to fund the *HMS Challenger* expedition, and then served as its chief scientist.

The crew measured the depth in about 400 places in all the large oceans. They also dragged scraping equipment over the seabed and examined the living things brought up from the deep. They collected enough data to fill fifty books!

Although this was just a tiny sample of the world's oceans, it was the first big expedition that was only about science. At the time, it was as expensive and ambitious as going to the Moon almost 100 years later!

The expedition taught us that the ocean floor was not flat, but an underwater landscape of mountains, flat plains, ridges, and trenches. More expeditions followed, and the new science of oceanography was here to stay.

EARTH'S IMMENSE OCEANS

# Mapping the deep

After the exciting discoveries of *HMS Challenger*, more expeditions followed. In the 1900s, all the data was used to produce the first maps of the ocean floor. Most famous of all are the drawings of Marie Tharp. They revealed what the ocean floor was REALLY like—not a flat nothingness, but an underwater seascape of towering mountain chains, giant volcanoes, and deep, dark trenches.

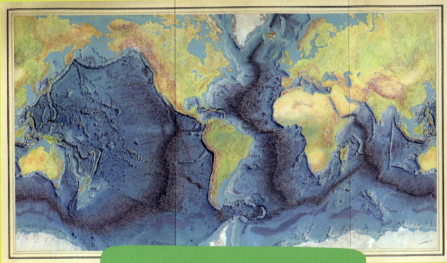

**1977 World Ocean Floor Map**

Marie helped create one of the most famous maps of all time—the 1977 World Ocean Floor Map. It was the first look at deep ocean floors around the world, and the mid-ocean ridges.

EXPLORING THE DEPTHS

# Speak like a scientist

## MID-OCEAN RIDGE

A mid-ocean ridge is a chain of volcanic mountains that runs across ocean basins. The Mid-Atlantic Ridge is part of the biggest mountain chain on Earth, stretching nearly 40,400 miles around the world.

## OCEAN HERO

### MARIE THARP

Oceanographic **cartographer**. Although women were not allowed on navy research ships at the time, she used data collected by others to hand-draw maps of the deep ocean floor.

Some of the mountains along mid-ocean ridges are so high, their tips poke out above the surface as islands. The country of Iceland is the tip of one of these mountains! As scientists investigated these ridges, they gathered evidence to support and understand Earth's tectonic plates.

EARTH'S IMMENSE OCEANS

Exploring the oceans had confirmed that Earth really has changed in the past—and is still changing, as the plates of the crust move about on top of a molten mantle.

## Diving deeper

It's possible to survey and sample the ocean floor from safely on board a ship but, just as on land, it's easier to understand something if you see it with your own eyes. By the mid-1800s, natural history museums were filling up with strange specimens collected from the sea floor. But this didn't tell people how these creatures lived.

To find out, we need equipment that allows us to breathe and stay warm underwater (and avoid getting crushed by the tremendous pressure of many miles of water pressing down from above!).

Many coastal communities have long histories of diving without equipment and know first-hand the hidden world beneath the waves, but free diving takes very special skill and is risky. The first diving suits and helmets were invented in the 1600s and 1700s.

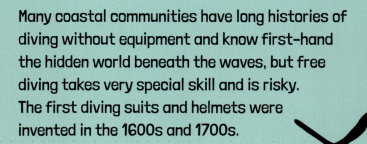

**EXPLORING THE DEPTHS**

The first submarines and **submersibles** made it possible to dive even deeper. By 1960, humans had visited the deepest known point on Earth—the Challenger Deep. Over the next few decades, ocean explorers such as Jacques Cousteau became just as famous as any explorer on land. Jacques taught himself marine biology and helped to invent the first Aqua-Lung for scuba diving, as well as a submarine and underwater cameras! Through his films and television programs he shared his love of the oceans with the world, inspiring many new ocean scientists. Jacques also helped to set up several underwater labs known as Continental Shelf Stations (Conshelf, for short), where scientists could live and work in the strange underwater world.

## OCEAN HERO

### JACQUES COUSTEAU

French naval officer who became a famous underwater explorer and **conservationist**.

69

EARTH'S IMMENSE OCEANS

# Amazing discoveries

By the late twentieth century, underwater exploration was booming! Each new exciting discovery wowed the world, including . . .

. . . deep-sea hydrothermal vents and their ecosystems of creatures that don't need sunlight to survive (see page 50)

. . . the first film of a living giant squid

. . . a fish that had only ever been seen in prehistoric fossil form

. . . and the discovery of the wreck of the world-famous ship, Titanic.

**EXPLORING THE DEPTHS**

Oceanographers became heroes, and one of the most famous—Kathryn Sullivan—was even selected to become an astronaut, traveling to space in 1984. Her experience of exploring the deep ocean floor was good training for walking in space! In 2020, Kathryn made headlines again after becoming the first woman to travel almost 6.8 miles to the deepest known point in the ocean—the Challenger Deep.

## OCEAN HERO

### KATHRYN SULLIVAN

**American oceanographer who became an astronaut.**

Aquarius Reef Base near Florida is one of the largest underwater labs today. Like an underwater International Space Station, it's also used to train astronauts! Despite all this work, 80% of the ocean's depths are still unexplored and unmapped. We still have more accurate maps of the surface of Mars and the Moon than we do the ocean floors!

# Using the Oceans

People have used the oceans as a source of food and materials for thousands of years. For most of this time these ocean resources were seen as limitless, but in the last 100 years we have learned they are not.

The world ocean is one of our main sources of food. Until the 1930s people focused on the seas around coasts, where this food was easiest to find. A simple law set out the territory of each coastal country—fixing a "three-mile line," roughly the distance that a cannon could fire!

Like the Moon or Mars, the open oceans beyond this—and the resources found there, from fish to whales—were thought of as belonging to everybody and nobody, and had no government.

## Who owns the oceans?

This changed in the 1900s, as people discovered that fish could run out and oil could be found under the sea floor. People began claiming ownership of the water and seabed much further from land, and

## USING THE OCEANS

conflicts began. The **United Nations** tried to establish fair laws of the sea. In 1983, it agreed that coastal countries would have the exclusive right to food and other resources found in the first 200 miles (322 km) of ocean around their coasts. These are known as Exclusive Economic Zones (or EEZ). However, anyone could use the surface of the ocean, even in an EEZ.

Today, there are also a growing number of Marine Protected Areas (or MPAs) where human activity above and below the surface is banned or limited to try to conserve resources, wildlife, or habitats.

People are still rushing to extract resources deep under the oceans.

EARTH'S IMMENSE OCEANS

## The ocean pantry

Around 57 million people work in ocean fishing, from small-scale fishers paddling dugout canoes along the shore, to the crews of massive super **trawlers** that literally suck fish out of the sea. Modern trawlers are like factories at sea, with high-tech mechanical and computer equipment for finding, catching, processing, and storing fish on board.

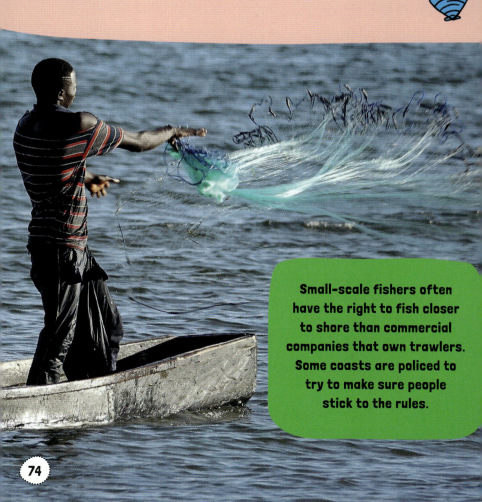

Small-scale fishers often have the right to fish closer to shore than commercial companies that own trawlers. Some coasts are policed to try to make sure people stick to the rules.

## USING THE OCEANS

Commercial fishing happens in every part of the ocean, except areas protected by law. Fish are caught from near the surface and from the very bottom. Many different types of boats, ships, and equipment are used to catch different types of fish—from nets or pots, to long lines with thousands of hooks. Many other types of sea animals are caught for food too, including crustaceans such a crabs, echinoderms such as sea cucumbers, mollusks such as mussels, and even sponges. People have also developed ways to "farm" sea creatures to speed up production of some species, known as **aquaculture**.

About 15% of protein eaten around the world comes from seafood. In many of the world's least wealthy countries, it's the main source of protein. Algae, including seaweed, is an important food in some coastal areas. Even people who don't eat seafood can depend on it. Fishmeal and algae is used to feed farm animals and fertilize crops. Algae are also used to make food additives.

edible algae

EARTH'S IMMENSE OCEANS

# Ocean power

As strange as it seems, oceans have a long history of heating and lighting homes! Before electricity was invented or fossil fuels were discovered, whale oil was burned in lamps to light homes, factories, and streets.

Whale oil smelled very fishy and in the late 1800s it was phased out in favor of mineral oil. But mineral oil, even when found on land, is also made from sea creatures!

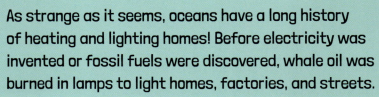

Over millions of years, ancient plankton sank to the bottom of oceans, became trapped between layers of sediment, and squeezed into a dense liquid rich in carbon and stored energy. We have been burning this fossil fuel to power transport, and light and heat homes, for more than a hundred years.

Mineral oil takes millions of years to form, so it is not a sustainable source of energy. Releasing its trapped carbon (as carbon dioxide) is also driving climate change. As people search for new sources of energy, they are once again turning to the oceans. Moving ocean water (tides, waves, and currents) can be harnessed to turn turbines and produce electricity.

**USING THE OCEANS**

Moving air (wind) can turn a wind turbine to generate electricity. Water is more than 800 times denser than air, so moving water provides a much bigger push!

> At a tidal barrage, rising or falling water is forced through turbines, which turn an electricity generator.

Ocean water also absorbs huge amounts of energy from sunlight, and this thermal energy can be used to generate electricity, too.

EARTH'S IMMENSE OCEANS

## Diverse resources

The ocean is the source of many other things used by humans. This includes water for countries with little fresh water; minerals such as salt; precious elements such as gold; and medicines and other useful chemicals extracted from living things.

Algae are common sources of food additives used to make ketchup and dairy products smooth and gloopy. Recently, fast food chains have even begun making the sauce sachets from algae! In the future, **biodegradable** products made from fast-growing algae may replace more and more plastics (which are made from mineral oil).

## Mining the abyss

Fossil fuels are regularly extracted from the ocean floor, and many other minerals can be found there too. Back in 1873, *HMS Challenger* (see page 64) collected strange lumps from the deep Pacific. They turned out to be rich in **manganese**—used to make both super-strong steel and light-but-bendy tin cans—and other useful metals such as cobalt and nickel.

Manganese nodules form over millions of years. Manganese from thermal vents that has dissolved in the oceans slowly starts to collect around a shark's

## USING THE OCEANS

tooth or a small piece of seashell. A manganese nodule can grow as big as a head of lettuce!

The ocean floor is littered with these nodules, but they have always been thought of as too expensive to mine. That is set to change soon.

In the future, **manganese nodules** will be picked up from the sea floor by machines and pumped to a ship through pipes. No such machines have been built yet.

riser pipe

armored hose

mining machine

lifting tool

nodule deposit

EARTH'S IMMENSE OCEANS

## The ocean highway

The way we live, eat, and shop today depends entirely on the oceans. Airplanes can fly people and cargo quickly from continent to continent, but this is expensive and energy-hungry. Water provides an upward-pushing force called the buoyant force, which cancels out some of an object's weight due to gravity. This means less energy is needed to move the object from place to place.

Each year, **12 billion tons of goods— around 80% of all international trade— is transported by ship.** That's the weight of a hippo for every single person in the world! These movements would simply not be possible by road, rail, or air—it would be too expensive and use too much energy.

The ocean highway is constantly in motion, with voyages carefully planned to get goods to shops, supermarkets, and factories just at the time they are needed. Most cargo travels along only a few major routes, which are as crowded as any highway on land. The number of huge cargo ships is growing all the time.

**USING THE OCEANS**

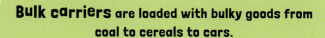

**Bulk carriers** are loaded with bulky goods from coal to cereals to cars.

**Tankers** carry liquids such as oil, chemicals, and liquid gas—even concentrated fruit juice!

These ships are **HUGE!** The biggest today are container ships 400 yards long (nearly the length of four football fields).

**Container ships** carry everything else, from toys to tennis shoes, packed into standard-sized containers that can be easily stacked, and then lifted off onto trains or lorries. This speeds up loading and unloading.

# Ocean traffic jam

Humans have carved great canals to link oceans and speed up journeys by months. Most of the time we take these epic engineering feats for granted, but they made headline news in 2021 when the container ship *Ever Given* (carrying 18,000 containers) got wedged in Egypt's Suez Canal for a week. It caused a traffic jam of more than 400 ships, and months of delays.

## Coastal communities

For people who live along or near coasts, the oceans are a source of other kinds of work—and play! As well as fishing, there are millions of jobs in transport at sea, aquaculture, marine science and biotech, ocean energy production, and tourism.

Almost half of the world's population lives within 90 miles of an ocean and even more visit the oceans for relaxation. The UN estimate that about 80% of all tourism takes place near coasts. The reason is that water is FUN!

On the sea you can splash around on boats, swim, and take part in water sports.

- You can **ski** and **surf** on the surface . . .
- . . . or **scuba dive** into hidden worlds.
- You can take a **fishing trip**, **splash** in the waves, or simply **sunbathe** on a beach.
- Some coastal communities depend on tourism for most of their jobs and income.

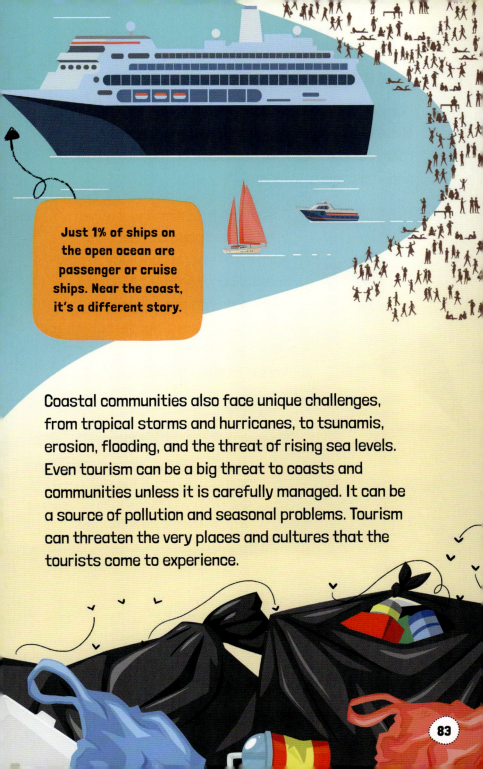

**Just 1% of ships on the open ocean are passenger or cruise ships. Near the coast, it's a different story.**

Coastal communities also face unique challenges, from tropical storms and hurricanes, to tsunamis, erosion, flooding, and the threat of rising sea levels. Even tourism can be a big threat to coasts and communities unless it is carefully managed. It can be a source of pollution and seasonal problems. Tourism can threaten the very places and cultures that the tourists come to experience.

EARTH'S IMMENSE OCEANS

# Oceans under pressure

Humans have been learning about the oceans for thousands of years, but only recently have we realized how much our activities are putting oceans under pressure.

**great auk**

One of the first signs was when whales (see page 59) became harder to hunt. In contrast to how coastal communities have lived in balance with the oceans for thousands of years, people saw that large-scale commercial activities quickly led to **over-exploitation**.

Species such as STELLAR'S SEA COW and the GREAT AUK became extinct in the 1700s and 1800s because humans hunted them for food.

**Stella's sea cow**

**USING THE OCEANS**

Most commercial whaling is now banned, and whale populations have recovered. However, people did not learn from history, and by the 1970s many **fish stocks** were disappearing too. By 2015, just two-thirds of the world's fish stocks were sustainable. The rest will soon run out unless action is taken.

It's not just about seafood—we are gradually learning how the loss of certain species has a knock-on effect on whole ecosystems. The coastal areas richest in fish, shellfish, and algae—such as coral reefs, seagrass meadows, and mangrove swamps—are also the most fragile and easily damaged by human activities. But the impact of human activities is seen everywhere in the ocean and affects processes that the entire world depends on—such as global carbon, nitrogen, and water cycles.

Putting oceans under pressure puts the entire planet under pressure.

EARTH'S IMMENSE OCEANS

## In the balance

We are still not taking enough action. In fact, things are getting worse as we expand our use of the ocean, with more fishing, pollution from land, and shipping than ever before. In 60% of the ocean, the impact of human activities, including the effects of climate change, is speeding up. There are plans for more offshore energy, deep-sea mining, and ocean farming—technologies that hope to tackle certain problems faced by humans but may cause new problems for the ocean. Some scientists have warned that human actions could soon push oceans beyond certain **tipping points**.

# Speak like a scientist

### TIPPING POINT

This is the point at which a certain amount of change triggers, starting a chain of events that lead triggers to unstoppable and irreversible change.

**USING THE OCEANS**

It's not just about what we take out of the ocean, but what we put in. Humans pollute the oceans in many different ways:

**Plastic pollution** injures and kills millions of sea creatures each year. It also disrupts ecosystems. About 80% of plastic in the ocean was thrown away on land.

**Heated water** from coastal industries can kill ocean animals and disrupt life cycles.

**Noise pollution** from shipping, mining, and energy extraction can confuse ocean animals, especially animals such as whales that rely on sound to communicate.

**Chemical pollution** from sewage and chemicals that run off land can poison ocean creatures directly, or upset the balance of the food chain.

**Radioactive pollution** from nuclear power stations, or weapons tests, can remain harmful for hundreds or even thousands of years.

Just one **spill** from an oil tanker or other cargo vessel can kill tens of thousands of ocean animals. There are 150 accidents a year.

EARTH'S IMMENSE OCEANS

Scientists such as Sylvia Earle have been uncovering the sources and impacts of pollution on ocean ecosystems and wildlife. Sometimes these can be unexpected. For example, scientists have recently found that microbes and other creatures are hitching rides on plastic pollution, and invading areas where they wouldn't normally live.

## OCEAN HERO

### SYLVIA EARLE

American oceanographer and explorer who has raised awareness of the threats of overfishing and pollution.

## Climate change

We are getting better and better at investigating the oceans. Today's ocean heroes include marine engineers who develop robots to monitor the oceans, and mathematicians and computer programmers who use the data to model how oceans change over time and make predictions for the future.

## USING THE OCEANS

They also include marine biologists who use genetics to better understand how ocean wildlife is being affected.

Over the last few decades, technology has helped scientists collect a **tsunami of evidence** that tells us **climate change is the biggest problem facing the oceans.**

Ocean observatories gather information from certain places in the ocean over many decades. There are eight main long-term observatories, and many smaller stations, scattered around the world. The data they collect tells us about natural patterns in ocean carbon cycling—and warns us when change is accelerating due to human activities.

Climate change is affecting each ocean ecosystem differently, but one of its most worrying impacts is changing the balance of chemicals dissolved in ocean. Water soaks up carbon dioxide from the air, so higher carbon dioxide emissions mean more dissolved carbon dioxide in seawater. This is making the oceans slightly more acidic.

More acidic water makes it harder for sea creatures to build their shells and skeletons, because the materials they use dissolve in acids. This includes the tiny phytoplankton that drive the carbon cycle and produce half the world's oxygen.

EARTH'S IMMENSE OCEANS

Every living thing is affected differently by climate change. Mussels are anchored in one place for most of their lives, so they cannot adapt easily to changes in temperature caused by global warming. More acidic ocean water also makes it harder for them to form their shells. In some parts of the world, mussel populations have dramatically fallen. This also affects populations that depend on farming the mussels for income.

## The future of oceans

Hundreds of years of exploration have shown us that oceans aren't just big bits of blue between continents. They're the engines of life on Earth!

Oceans have shaped human history, and we rely on them every day for food, energy, trade, transport, and fun. We are beginning to understand how our activities shape the oceans in return—for good and for bad. But we need to get even better at learning from the science of today and the stories of the past, and live alongside oceans in a sustainable way.

**New Zealand fur seals** were hunted for fur and meat for more than 600 years, and by the early 1900s populations were very small. They have been protected for the last forty years and today more than a million fur seals live around Australia.

We can all play a role in protecting the ocean, no matter how far from the coast we live. If you are interested in exploring, understanding, and protecting the oceans, you could even become an ocean scientist, conservationist, or policy maker yourself! The first step is to keep studying chemistry, physics, biology, geography, and mathematics at school. These subjects will give you the skills to work in oceanography and become an **ocean hero of the future.**

# Glossary

**algae** simple green plants that include seaweeds and single-celled microbes; some types of bacteria are also nicknamed algae

**amino acids** simple chemicals that are the building blocks of proteins

**aquaculture** farming marine animals or plants for food

**arthropod** a member of a group of animals with a segmented body and a hard exoskeleton that includes insects, spiders, and crustaceans

**baleen** horn-like plates in the mouth of certain whales, used to filter food out of the water

**biodegradable** can be broken down naturally by bacteria, fungi, and other living things

**bioluminescence** light made by living things

**cartographer** a professional mapmaker

**climate** the typical pattern of weather in a place over time

**cnidarian** a member of a group of animals that includes jellyfish, corals, and sea anemones

**conservationist** a person who takes action to protect and preserve environments, and the wildlife that live in them

**crustacean** a member of a group of animals that includes crabs, lobsters, and barnacles

**cyanobacteria** a group of bacteria that can harvest the energy in sunlight to make their own food

**data** facts, figures, or other information that has been collected in order to find something out

**dense** closely packed together

**denser** has a higher density

**detritivore** an animal that eats dead organic matter and waste that drifts down from higher in the water column

**dissolved** broken up into such small pieces it becomes part of a liquid